LET'S VISIT ISRAEL

Let's visit
ISRAEL

DISCARD

GARRY LYLE

BURKE

First published October 1972
Second revised edition 1984

ACKNOWLEDGEMENTS

The author and publishers are grateful to the following individuals and organizations for
permission to reproduce copyright photographs in this book:
 Art Directors Photo Library; E. Clay; Arnold Cohen; Colorific!; Geoffrey Craig;
 Douglas Dickens; Israel Government Tourist Office; Jewish National Fund;
 Youth Aliya.
The cover illustration of the Western Wall is reproduced by permission of Picturepoint
Limited, London.

CIP data
Lyle, Garry
 Let's visit Israel. – 2nd ed.
 ① Israel – Social life and customs – Juvenile literature
 I. Title
 956.94'05   DS112

ISBN 0 222 01027 4

Burke Publishing Company Limited
Pegasus House, 116-120 Golden Lane, London EC1Y 0TL, England.
Burke Publishing (Canada) Limited
Registered Office: 20 Queen Street West, Suite 3000, Box 30, Toronto, Canada M5H 1V5.
Burke Publishing Company Inc.
Registered Office: 333 State Street, PO Box 1740, Bridgeport, Connecticut 06601, U.S.A.
Filmset in "Monophote" by Green Gates Studios Ltd., Hull, England.
Printed in Singapore by Tien Wah Press (Pte) Ltd.

Contents

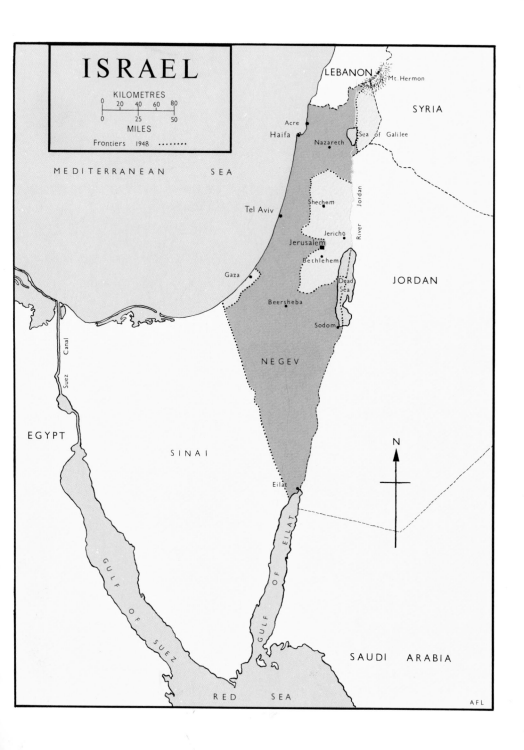

ISRAEL

KILOMETRES
0   20   40   60   80
0   25   50
MILES

Frontiers   1948 ....

MEDITERRANEAN   SEA

LEBANON
Mt. Hermon
SYRIA

Acre
Haifa
Nazareth
Sea of Galilee

Shechem

Tel Aviv

Jericho
Jerusalem
Bethlehem

Gaza

Dead
Sea
JORDAN

Beersheba

Sodom

NEGEV

EGYPT

SINAI

N

Eilat

GULF   OF   SUEZ

GULF   OF   EILAT

SAUDI   ARABIA

RED   SEA

AFL

A Biblical scene in modern times—a Bedouin Arab leading his flock
in the Negev

Israel Old, Israel New

Among the paper scattered over our floors one Christmas, two pieces caught my attention because they mentioned the name Israel in a sharply contrasting way. The first was a square of gift-wrapping, printed with a pattern of shepherds in the clothes of Bible times. They were standing with their sheep on a bare, frosty hillside, looking up at a very bright star as they sang "Born is the King of Israel". And that, of course, is how most of us first meet the name Israel. Christmas carols and Christmas Bible stories tell us of the birth of Jesus, and Israel was the nation to which Jesus belonged.

Other Bible stories give us pictures of the people Israel—also called Hebrews or Jews—through two thousand years of their history. We see them as a family of tented herdsmen on the dry plains north of Arabia, moving their animals from well to well and dreaming that they will one day settle in a land of their own, "a land flowing with milk and honey", as the Bible calls it. We see them as slaves in Egypt and as hungry refugees in the desert of Sinai. We see them at last winning a foothold in their "land flowing with milk and honey"—a small rugged country at the eastern end of the Mediterranean Sea. We see them becoming a nation of farmers and craftsmen and traders, a nation trying to live in peace under just laws, and guided by great religious teachers. We see them settled in the land for more than a thousand years, sometimes powerful and prosperous, more often divided and oppressed, but always holding on.

That brings us to the time of Jesus, to shepherds watching a star over Bethlehem nearly two thousand years ago. And, for some people, the picture has scarcely changed since. In their minds, the land of Israel is still as it was when Jesus taught by the Sea of Galilee and walked the dusty road southward to the great Temple in Jerusalem. So they are often a little surprised when they find something that shows them a newer picture. That other piece of paper on our floor at Christmas, for instance. It was a very modern-looking label, printed with a bright blue band across an even brighter bunch of cherries. And along the band were the words *Cherry Creme Chocolate— Made by the Nazareth Candy Co. Ltd., Nazareth, Israel.*

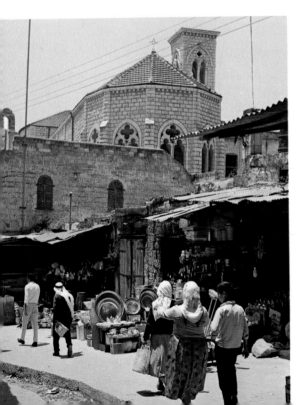

A street in Nazareth

A signpost in three languages: Hebrew, Arabic and English

A candy factory in Nazareth, the village where Jesus worked as a carpenter? Yes, indeed. There is also a very big textile factory; and, not far away, you can find people making machinery and plastics, and assembling cars and trucks. Some of their products are carried along smooth motor-roads to the busy new seaport of Haifa, thirty kilometres (nineteen miles) east of Nazareth. From there, they travel abroad in Israel's own fleet of modern cargo-ships—some of them built in Israel and powered by oil from Israel's own wells.

Nazareth and Haifa merely start the surprises. The land of Israel can spring much bigger ones on people who take all their pictures from the Bible.

11

Visitors learn very quickly why Theodor Herzl, the nine-teenth-century Austrian-Jewish writer, gave it the name *Altneuland*, which means *Oldnewland*. It is old because it is the homeland of a very ancient nation. It is new because it is the territory of a very young state. And the young state belongs so clearly to the twentieth century that you can hardly believe you have come to the land of the Bible when you see a shoreline of skyscrapers and oil-tanks as you sail into Haifa Bay, or look down at the teeming new city of Tel Aviv as you fly into the international airport at Lod.

But that is only a first impression. Links with the Bible are still there, and very strongly there. The four million people of the young state belong mainly to the ancient nation. They speak the Hebrew language in which the Old Testament of the Bible was written. Most of them follow the religion of the Old Testament. Laws, customs and traditions going back to the Old Testament touch their daily lives. And all of them share with the Old Testament people the belief that their land is worth holding, and will be held while they have power to do some-thing about it.

Strangers have sometimes wondered what makes the land worth holding. It is very small—less than five hundred kilo-metres (three hundred miles) long, nowhere more than about one hundred kilometres (sixty miles) wide, and at one point only ten kilometres (six miles) wide. Much of it is what the Bible calls wilderness—rocky hills and arid valleys that often merge into desert. Much of the rest has been made fertile only at great expense of labour and money. It is short of water and, until recently, it appeared to have hardly any useful minerals. Its sandy coastline lacks natural harbours, and is open to wild winds and winter storms. Its climate is usually very pleasant for visitors, but can be either over-hot or over-cool (depending on the time of year) for people who have to work in it. Many of its neighbours are, and always have been, unfriendly. And, because of its position near the neck between Asia and Africa, it has often been a corridor and a battleground for the armies of stronger countries. In fact, to the early Hebrew settlers it was "a land flowing with milk and honey" only by comparison with the harsh, hungry lands through which they had been wandering. And it had much less to offer their descendants who began the modern state of Israel, because it had been misused and neglected for centuries.

Then why *is* it worth holding? A citizen of the modern state

Loading oranges in Haifa port

Today roads go through the wilderness. This is a section of the road to Sodom

might answer by saying *"Ein brera"*, which is the Hebrew for "There is no alternative". But he would say it with a smile. It is true that many citizens of the modern state were driven out of other countries by persecution or poverty, or simply by the feeling that they were not welcome. It is also true that some of them could have found no refuge except the state of Israel. But there is more to it than that. Just how much more, we may begin to see if we look a little more closely into the story of their ancestors.

14

The People Israel

The Bible story of Noah's Ark tells us that a great flood once destroyed the whole human race, except Noah and his family. Noah had three sons named Shem, Ham and Japheth. And the story goes on to say that all people born after the flood were members of one of three groups—one group descended from Shem, one from Ham, and one from Japheth.

Nowadays we know that the differing kinds and colours of human beings cannot be explained so simply. But that does not mean that there was no flood. Nor does it mean that what is now a very big and mixed racial group could not have been a very small one—perhaps a single family—in the far-distant past. So it could well be a fact that the group we call the Semites began as the family of a man called Shem, who survived a disastrous flood long before the Bible story was written.

Many centuries later, when the Jews were settled in the land that is now called Israel, the family of Shem had become a group of nations—mainly the Phoenicians, the Assyrians, some Arabian peoples and the Jews themselves. They all lived side by side in south-west Asia. They were similar in appearance, in language, in clothing and in many of their customs. But they differed—or rather the Jews differed from the rest—in their ideas about gods.

Like other ancient peoples, most of the Semites believed that gods existed in large numbers. They also believed that their many gods could be persuaded to help or harm human beings, but were not much concerned about the behaviour of human beings. What made the Jews different was a strong belief in one god, only one god, who did concern himself with the behaviour of human beings.

This led them to another idea uncommon in the ancient world—the idea of human dignity. They saw each human being as a separate and special person, with rights and responsibilities under laws which expected all human beings to behave with justice, compassion and respect for each other's worth. For that, the whole of mankind is in debt to them. Through the Christian and Muslim religions as well as their own, their ideas spread widely, and did much to shape what we think of as civilized living.

The Bible traces the beginning of their ideas—and the beginning of their nation—to a man named Abraham. Abraham was a wandering herdsman who led his family and his animals in search of a land that they could call their own. He lived nearly four thousand years ago, but if we think of him

Acre is a town with both Christian and Muslim traditions. This is the mosque of Al-Jazzar

as someone rather like the leader of a small group of Bedouin Arabs today we will not be far wrong. It was as a party of visiting desert nomads that his people first pitched their tents in the "promised land". They called it the "promised land" because Abraham believed that God wanted him and his descendants to have it for ever—which helps to explain why the Jews have always been so anxious to hold it. But it was a very long time before they could call it their own. Abraham and his son Isaac died there, but they were never more than migrant strangers. And famine forced the large family of his

17

grandson Jacob to move into Egypt. Jacob had taken another name, Israel, which means "the strong one of God". So the descendants of his twelve sons became known as the twelve tribes of Israel, or the people Israel.

The people Israel—or at any rate large numbers of them— seem to have lived in Egypt for at least three hundred years, many of them as slave labourers. But they never lost the belief that Abraham's promised land would one day be theirs. Nor did they lose the chance of going there when the great law-giver Moses arranged their escape into Sinai. Led first by Moses and then by his successor Joshua, they came (after much danger and suffering) to the River Jordan, crossed it near the ancient city of Jericho, and slowly spread their settlements over the whole land from Dan in the mountainous north to Beersheba in the desert south.

They were not allowed to settle without a struggle. There were other Semites in the land, not all of them willing to share it with newcomers. In the southern half of the long coastal plain lived some immigrants of a different race, the Philistines. The Philistines had come there by sea, perhaps from the island of Crete, while the Jews were in Egypt. Although they were content with their coastland settlements, they did not like to feel that other people were filling the hill country behind them. So they tried to drive the Jews out.

The Jews responded by making the hill country into a kingdom. Until then, each of the twelve tribes had governed itself and acted to suit itself, with advice from religious and

18

military leaders called judges. But many setbacks showed them that they would have to unite if they were to check not only their Semitic enemies but also the warlike and well-armed Philistines. So in the years around 1000 B.C. the twelve tribes began to act as one nation under their first two kings—Saul and David. (According to Christian belief, David was an ancestor of Mary the mother of Jesus. That is why Christmas carols speak of the baby Jesus as king of Israel.)

David is one of the best-known figures in Jewish history, because of his duel with the giant Philistine, Goliath. He is also famous as the writer as some of the songs which the Bible calls psalms. But his real importance to the Jewish nation came from two achievements that are less well-known. He secured the

A view of Jericho

land for his people by ending the long struggles with their Semitic enemies and the Philistines. And he made the hilltop city of Jerusalem the capital of his kingdom.

To the Jews, Jerusalem had been a special place and a holy place since the time of Abraham. It was an old city even then. Abraham had been kindly welcomed there when he first arrived in the promised land. Because of that, the descendants of Abraham began to link the city with the God of Abraham. King David strengthened the link by building an altar there, and by bringing into the city the Ark of the Covenant, the sacred golden box in which his people kept a copy of their first laws, the Ten Commandments. David's son, the wise and wealthy King Solomon, adorned the city with a magnificent temple built to house the Ark and other sacred objects. And, from that time onward, Jerusalem became the centre of Jewish life and of the Jewish faith.

In the peaceful years of Solomon, the people Israel prospered as they never had before. But they also became disunited. When Solomon died, two rival kings took his place. One ruled in the north, one ruled in the south. And neither kingdom took much notice of the wise men—the prophets of the Bible—who warned them that their behaviour might cause them to lose the gains of a thousand years. So both kingdoms grew weaker and weaker.

The northern kingdom, which had taken the name Israel, was the first to fall. In 721 B.C. Assyrians from the east overran it, added it to their empire, and took most of its people away

20

into captivity. Nobody knows what happened to them, but they probably died as slaves.

That left the people Israel with only half the promised land —the territory of the southern kingdom. The southern kingdom was called Judah after the tribe of King David. Because it was now the only kingdom left to the people Israel, the world began thinking of the whole people as Judaeans, later shortened to Jews. But Judah too was conquered by invaders from an eastern empire. They were the Babylonians, who sacked Jerusalem, destroyed Solomon's temple, and moved many of Judah's people eastward to a long exile in Babylon.

The exile ended when Babylon itself was conquered. It fell to yet another eastern empire, Persia, in 538 B.C. And because the Persians wanted friends in countries further west they let the Jews go home. Back in the promised land, the returned exiles built a new temple and new walls round Jerusalem. But although the Persians usually allowed them to govern themselves, they had little real independence. And they lost even that when invading Greeks from Europe replaced the Persians.

At this time, they were also in danger of losing the religion and the ancient laws and customs which shaped their whole way of living. So they rose to fight for them under a family of national leaders named the Maccabees. The rising succeeded. For the first time in centuries, the Jews were their own masters in their own land. But not for long. At the end of the Bible period, they were facing a struggle with the world's newest and greatest empire, Rome. This struggle left them without an

The Romans improved the country's water supply by means of aqueducts like this one

independent, Jewish-governed homeland for nearly two thousand years.

Under the Romans and the puppet kings who ruled for them, the land of the Jews looked prosperous. The water supply was improved. New cities were built, with new roads between them and new harbour works to link them by sea with Rome. But there was little pleasure for the Jews in the new look of their land. They were heavily over-taxed to pay for it, and saw most of their country's wealth going to foreigners who showed little respect for Jewish beliefs and customs.

Thus, Jesus was born among a deprived and discontented

people, and grew up in a country that was never very far from rebellion. He himself was thought of as a rebel. But it was not until about thirty years after he died that the world's smallest country made its last stand against the world's biggest empire. The stand lasted seven years, and ended with thousands of Jews slaughtered, thousands more taken to Rome as prisoners, the temple wrecked, burnt and robbed of its treasures, Jerusalem destroyed, and the last of the rebels killing themselves in the great rock fort at Massada when they knew that they could hold out no longer.

Massada fell in A.D. 73. From then onward there were more Jews outside their homeland than in it. They spread and settled all over the civilized world, and very often helped to make it more civilized. But they never lost interest in the land of Israel, nor shed the belief that it would one day be theirs again. Year after year, Jewish families everywhere kept up the religious festival called Passover, in memory of the time when Moses led the people Israel out of Egypt. Year after year, at the Passover meal, the head of each family would say *"Le shana haba bi Yerushalaim"*, which in Hebrew means "Next year in Jerusalem", for the traditional celebration of the festival had always been in the temple in Jerusalem to which thousands of pilgrims went each year.

The rock fortress of Massada. (Note the hard-baked soil in the foreground)

The State of Israel

"Next year" was a long time coming. The Romans did their best to make sure that it would never come. They even re-named the country Palestine, in memory of Israel's old enemies the Palestini, or Philistines. But the Romans themselves had left by about A.D. 400. Greek rulers followed them; and after the Greeks came the Persians. The Persians gave way to Arabs, the Arabs to Turks. Then came Crusaders from the countries of western Europe, and finally Turks again.

But, whoever ruled the land, there were always Jews in it. Some belonged to families who had never gone away. They had survived the troubles with the Romans and kept up pockets of Jewish life—sometimes very big pockets—among the changing mixture of strangers. Others were foreign settlers in their own homeland. They had come back to it from countries where their ancestors had been living—often unhappily—since Roman times and earlier. To many of them the country had given a cold welcome. The rulers often oppressed them. There was little work in the towns. The best of the farmland had been taken by others, mainly Arabs from countries near by. And some of the newcomers could stay only because friends abroad were glad to give money towards maintaining a Jewish community in the promised land.

The community was known by the Hebrew name *Yishuv* ("Community"). For nearly fifteen centuries it grew very slowly, and sometimes shrank. But from 1877 to 1914—the years towards the end of Turkish rule—it was vastly enlarged by a rush of newcomers, mainly from the countries of eastern Europe. Partly because they held fast to their religion and customs, but mainly because it suited unscrupulous rulers to blame them in times of trouble, Jews in some foreign countries had often been cruelly persecuted and forced to live in great discomfort. For many in eastern Europe, life had become unbearable. Their only hope was emigration. And, though the brightest possible future seemed to lie in America, thousands chose to turn homeward and join the Yishuv.

At first, they made their own way to Palestine, sometimes singly, sometimes in families, sometimes as small groups of neighbours. And if any thought that they were going to a "land flowing with milk and honey" they soon found otherwise. The Turks had been interested only in holding Palestine. They did little to look after it. So huge areas of farmland and woodland had become marsh and desert. And that was the only land available to newcomers who had little money and less knowledge of farming. But they did have the will to make a lasting home for themselves. In time, they also had help from wealthy Jews abroad. By 1900, Palestine had seventeen new and successful farming villages.

Meanwhile, the Zionist movement had been founded by the Austrian-Jewish writer Theodor Herzl. The Zionist movement took its name from Mount Zion in Jerusalem, which to Jews was a symbol of their faith. Its aim was to have Palestine returned to the Jews as an independent state for those who

**Acre harbour today
—Israeli fishing
boats set against
a Crusader
background**

wished to live there. While it was trying to win support from
the nations of the world, it encouraged and helped new settlers.
By 1914, there were eighty-five thousand people in the
Yishuv, and many more wanting to join it.

Independence seemed to be coming closer, too. Turkey
fought on the losing side in the First World War so, after 1918,
Palestine was no longer under Turkish rule. The Jews hoped
that the winning nations would see this as the right time to
make the country into a Jewish state. In fact, the winning

27

nations had already agreed to do so. But some of the Palestinian Arabs objected, often violently. They were supported by the governments of some neighbouring Arab countries. Those countries were able to influence Britain, which was governing Palestine on behalf of the League of Nations. Though the Yishuv continued to grow and prosper, hopes of independence had faded when the Second World War began in 1939.

The war changed the picture again. In the most monstrous of all persecutions, six million Jews of Germany and eastern Europe were murdered at the orders of the German government. But millions more survived, and many of those were unwilling to stay in Europe. Many too were "displaced persons"—refugees who could find no home in Europe. Now, more than ever, the Jewish people needed their national home. And the need was recognized by the United Nations Organization, which had replaced the League of Nations.

The Arabs still resisted, and now there were many more of them. As the Yishuv had grown, so had Palestine's standard of living, and Arabs from poorer countries near by had come to share in it. They were afraid that a Jewish government would drive them from their new homes. The neighbouring Arab countries encouraged their fears. There was violence on both sides. The United Nations Organization tried to satisfy both by dividing the country between them. Even that was not enough for the Arab leaders. They decided that the only solution was "to drive the Jews into the sea." And they tried to do so when Britain gave up the responsibility for governing Palestine.

The Yishuv, now more than 650,000 people, was not dismayed. On the day that British government ended—14th May, 1948—the Jewish leader David Ben-Gurion declared that Palestine had become the independent state of Israel. Reading from a proclamation of independence, he told the other nations of the world:

"The State of Israel . . . will devote itself to developing the Land for the good of all its inhabitants. It will rest upon foundations of liberty, justice and peace as envisioned by the Prophets of Israel. It will maintain complete equality of social and political rights for all its citizens, without distinction of creed, race or sex. It will guarantee freedom of religion and conscience, of language, education and culture. It will safeguard the Holy Places of all religions. It will be loyal to the principles of the United Nations Charter."

The clear promises of the proclamation were still not enough for the leaders of the Palestine Arabs and the neighbouring Arab countries. Their armies were already surrounding the Jewish part of Palestine. They had already told Arabs living in the Jewish part to leave. Now their armies attacked.

Seven months later, they were asking for peace. Far from being in the sea, the citizens of the Jewish state—Israelis as they were now called—had driven the invaders back to the borders, and looked capable of driving them further. But they accepted an armistice which left parts of old Palestine, including some of Jerusalem, in the hands of the invaders.

A view of the Weizmann Institute, a centre for post-graduate and research work in all fields of science. It is named after the first President of the State, Chaim Weizmann, who was a distinguished chemist as well as a statesman

From those parts, some of the Arabs who had left Israel came back, often with help from the Israelis. Like the Arabs who had stayed, they settled down as citizens of the new state, and the new state settled down to the task of "developing the land for the good of all its inhabitants". The task has been done very well. After twenty years, a country neglected for centuries and then ravaged by war was supporting three million people at a high standard of living. And through all those twenty years the Israelis were rarely allowed to live and work in peace. Palestinian Arabs who had not come back made guerilla raids across the borders. Neighbouring Arab countries interfered with Israel's foreign trade. In 1956, one of them—

Egypt—massed troops and built up attack bases in Sinai, immediately south of Israel. That led to fighting in which the Israeli citizen army had a startlingly swift success. In only a few days, it cleared the Sinai frontier of Egyptian bases, and then moved down to the Straits of Tiran, at the mouth of the Gulf of Eilat. There, it destroyed the base from which Egypt had been closing the gulf and the valuable port of Eilat to Israel's sea-trade.

Guerilla raids continued. So did attempts to injure Israel by more peaceful means. But there was no further threat of a full-scale invasion until 1967. Then, with backing from most

A view of Rishon-le-Zion, the chief wine-growing centre of Israel, showing the sandy soil of the coast. Further inland are the fertile wheatfields and orchards which have been developed from what was once neglected land

other neighbouring countries, Egypt moved a very large part of her army and air force into Sinai. At the same time, the Egyptian president broadcast: "Egypt, with all its resources—human, economic and scientific—is ready to plunge into a total war that will be the end of Israel."

The result was the famous Six-day War—so called because it took a much smaller Israeli force just six days to clear the enemy from all its frontiers, and to occupy not only the whole of Sinai, but also the parts of old Palestine which had been held by Egypt and Jordan since 1948 and some of the part of Syria called the Golan Heights. Later, after other unsuccessful attacks by Egypt and Syria in 1973, Israel moved further into the Golan Heights and, in 1981, put the area under Israeli law.

Those territories are more than three times the size of Israel proper—about 66,560 square kilometres (26,000 square miles) as against about 20,000 square kilometres (8,000 square miles). They include some land that is richly productive, some land that cannot become productive without long and expensive attention, and the older part of Jerusalem—the part sacred not only to Jews, but also to the 650,000 Muslim and Christian Israelis. However, the occupied territories are now about 60,000 square kilometres (23,000 square miles) smaller than they were in the 1970s. When the U.S.A. persuaded Israel and Egypt to sign a peace treaty in 1979, Israel agreed to give Sinai back to Egypt. By 1982 Israel had done so.

At that time, Israel was being threatened by terrorist attacks from a large number of Arab guerrilla fighters who had established bases in Lebanon, dangerously close to the border between Lebanon and Israel. These guerrillas also caused a great deal of trouble—including serious fighting and destruction—within Lebanon, and the Lebanese government was unable to control them. The Israelis therefore began a series of attacks across the border, in alliance with a group of Lebanese who were also opposed to the guerrillas, and had suffered much at their hands.

Then, when guerrilla activities continued, Israel launched a full-scale invasion of Lebanon, and over-ran the southern half of the country. By the end of 1983, many of the guerrillas had left Lebanon altogether, and most of the others had been pushed back so far that they were no longer a danger to Israel. The Israeli forces then began to withdraw, but they are still occupying a strip of Lebanese territory in the south, along the border.

Although Israel occupies that strip and the other captured territories, she does not own them. In time, she may agree to share, or even to give back, at least some of them. But she faces the uncomfortable fact that they have been used—and still could be used—in attempts to destroy her. And so she believes that she cannot safely let them go until she is sure of the "just and lasting peace" which the United Nations Organization is trying to arrange between her and the Arab countries.

Meanwhile, the citizens of the occupied territories are allowed as far as possible to live by their own laws, and in all other ways are governed and treated as though they were citizens of Israel.

The Citizens of Israel

Next to the human population, the most noticeable inhabitants of Israel are prickly pears. Called *sabra* by the Israelis, the prickly pear is a big cactus with flat, prickly leaves and reddish fruit whose tough skin is also prickly. It can look after itself and give a good crop of tasty fruit in poor growing conditions, and so was very useful to the pioneer settlers of modern Israel. They thought so highly of it that they began using the word *sabra* as a pet name for their children. Now, *sabra* has become the general name for any Israeli who was born in Israel.

Nowadays the sabras—nearly half of Israel's population— say that the name suits them very well. And visitors are inclined to agree. Like the sabra fruit, sabra Israelis are rather

A view of Galilee, with the Sea of Galilee in the background. The cactus in the foreground is the one called "sabra"; its fruit is prickly on the outside but sweet and tender inside

Typical of the contrasts in Israel's population, the boy on the left is an Indian Jew from Cochin on the Malabar coast; the man on the right is a "sabra" born of Russian parents.

rough and tough on the outside. Visitors at first find them pushing, not very considerate, and a little curt in their manners. But—also like the sabra fruit—they prove to be pleasant indeed once you are past the outer toughness. It is a very unlucky visitor who leaves Israel without discovering how friendly, kind and considerate they can be.

Their parents and grandparents born in other countries are just as friendly, kind and considerate. They are much more likely to show it before you get to know them—to be as gentle and attentive on the surface as the sabras are rough and offhand. An immigrant Israeli would probably stand back to let you have the only spare seat on a bus. His sabra grandson would probably shove past you and grab it for himself.

What makes the difference? Perhaps it is partly the fact that sabras are different people. An immigrant Israeli may come from a country where his ancestors have been settled for hundreds of years. He brings with him ideas, habits, language, perhaps even physical appearance which he owes to the people of that country. But in Israel he meets and mixes with people whose ancestors have lived in dozens of other countries. He may marry one of those people. And their children may marry people with backgrounds different from those of either parent. So a sabra could easily be the grandchild of people born in Warsaw, New York, Tunis and Baghdad. And, with such a confusing mixture of traditions in their family lives and their national life, sabras tend to be impatient about them all. Some, too, are inclined to be impatient about their common Jewish traditions. They like to feel that they are a new people, making their own Israeli traditions against their own Israeli background. They are also very conscious that it is up to them to keep Israel thriving and developing. And, with war a constant danger, that gives them the tremendous job of building their country and defending it at the same time. We can hardly blame them if they seem to be people in a hurry, offhand in manner and over-ready to push on.

Of course, the way of life that they follow is not, and cannot be, entirely new. Much of it is based on ideas brought in from other countries. For instance the Knesset, Israel's democratically elected parliament, is chosen by the proportional representation voting system used in Germany and France, and is very like the British House of Commons in the way in which it conducts its business. The principles of Israel's very fair and open legal system owe something to Britain, too. And the president of Israel, though elected, has much the same position and powers as Britain's reigning king or queen. He holds the presidency by consent of parliament, but does not support or represent any particular political party. His task is to represent, and to act for, all the people.

Also, much of the Israeli way of life is decided by the interests and the needs of settlers from other countries, who are still arriving at the rate of about thirty thousand a year. Education is an important example, though at first glance there seems to be little unusual about education in Israel. Perhaps there are more new schools than elsewhere; and a wider variety of face-types among the pupils than many

Israeli schoolchildren are like schoolchildren the world over; they cannot resist a look at the photographer, or a chance for a chat when the teacher's attention is elsewhere. This classroom is in a children's village

Arab children who live
on a new housing estate
near Haifa, in contrast to
their ancestors who
were nomads

visitors are used to. And they may be surprised to find that in most schools the day begins at eight o'clock and ends at one o'clock. But everything else is familiar—attendance between the ages of five and sixteen, ball games and sweets and noise in the playgrounds, a rush for the gates after the last lesson. It is only when a visitor looks at a school time-table that he finds something to surprise him, and the surprise comes from the number of language lessons.

Israel's national language is Hebrew, so everyone learns that, naturally enough. But about 600,000 of the people are Palestinian Arabs who have become Israeli citizens. And their language is Arabic. So Arab children must learn their Hebrew as a foreign language. Hebrew is a foreign language to the children of new settlers, too. They arrive in Israel speaking Polish, English, Yiddish (a German dialect with some Hebrew words in it), Russian or any of twenty other languages. But hardly any of them know any Hebrew. As schoolbooks are written in Hebrew and lessons taught in Hebrew, they must learn some Hebrew before they can learn anything else. It is not an easy language to learn, either. Its alphabet and grammar are not at all like the alphabets and grammars of English and the other languages of Europe. And it is not only written from right to left on the page, but also from right to left in the book—which means that the first page of a book in Hebrew is what we would call the last. Try writing and reading a little of your own language like that, and you will see why beginners in

One of Israel's most modern school buildings

Hebrew sometimes think that they are standing on their heads.

But learning the language is a matter of *ein brera* for settlers' children. Perhaps because there really is no alternative, they often learn it remarkably quickly. The many Hebrew-speaking children who learn Arabic usually learn that language quickly, too. But that is not so remarkable. Both Hebrew and Arabic are Semitic languages and, although they are written in different alphabets, they have much in common. For instance, the Hebrew words for "hello" and "year" are *shalom* (which really means "peace") and *shana*, while in Arabic the same words are *salaam* and *sana*. If you say both pairs of words, you will see that the gap between them is even narrower than it may look in print, and the gap is just as narrow at many other points in the two languages.

Even allowing for the links between Hebrew and Arabic, all that may seem quite enough language-learning for any school. But Israeli schools must go further. More than half of Israel's exports (mainly polished diamonds, chemicals, fruit, fruit products and other foodstuffs, textiles and tyres) are sent to the countries of western Europe and North America. More than three-quarters of Israel's imports come from those countries. So do most of the tourists who visit Israel to see the holy and historical places, to meet Israeli relations, to find out what is really happening in the new state, to enjoy the many entertainments offered by lively cities like Tel Aviv, or just to have a warm holiday. And, as very few people in Europe and the

40

U.S.A. speak Hebrew, nearly all Israeli children learn English in their secondary school years, and some learn French, too. They may well need both—and also their Hebrew and Arabic —if they work in foreign business or the tourist industry when they leave school.

Of course, their parents and elders have the language problem, too. New settlers can neither do much work nor take much part in community life until they have learnt Hebrew, so they go to school after the children have come home. Or rather they go to school if they have not been called up for compulsory military service. If they have been called up, they learn their Hebrew while they are in the army.

In Israel, all citizens are entitled to vote at parliamentary elections after their eighteenth birthday. With the vote come other responsibilities. Compulsory military service is one of them. That is how Israel manages to keep a well-trained defence force ready for the attacks which must always be expected while her neighbours remain unfriendly. Because the compulsory service period is a fairly long one—two and a half years or more for men and two years for unmarried women— the army uses some of the time to get new settlers ready for civilian life.

For many of them, that means a good deal more than learning to speak and read Hebrew. The Jews who shaped the state of Israel were mainly European Jews or sabra children of European Jews. Their standards of government, education, employment, housing, hygiene and personal comfort were

Children in the kibbutz dormitory

European standards. And they set similar standards for Israel. So newcomers from Europe find themselves in fairly familiar surroundings. But for many years most new settlers came from other continents, and often from areas with very different standards. Fifty thousand arrived in a single year from one area alone—the Yemen, in south-west Arabia. They were brought to Israel by a special air service called Operation Magic Carpet. Hardly any had flown before; some had never seen an aircraft. And they were no more familiar with many other things in the everyday life of Israel. Nor are most of the settlers from Jewish groups who have lived for centuries in parts of central Asia, India and the countries of north Africa. Before they can settle down in Israel, they must learn how to live in Israel. And the many who begin their life in Israel with compulsory military service are taught by the army. The lessons can include everything from understanding trade unions and traffic signs to using beds and lavatories—which explains why the army has been called the biggest school in Israel.

Operation Magic Carpet was largely arranged by an organization called the Jewish Agency. The Jewish Agency began as a branch of the League of Nations, and now works with the Israeli government, bringing in new settlers, educating them for life in Israel, and helping them to become farmers. The work is paid for mainly by gifts from Jews and friends of

The Jews of Yemen have a proud heritage and are skilled at embroidery and silver-smithing. This Yemeni bridal dress now forms an attractive exhibit in the Israel Museum in Jerusalem

The dining-room at Yemin Orde. This Youth Aliyah village is named after Orde Wingate, a distinguished British officer who was an active supporter of the Zionist cause

Israel all over the world. Much of it is done by a branch of the agency called Youth Aliyah. *Aliyah* is the Hebrew word for "ascent". The Bible uses this word when it speaks of people "going up" to Jerusalem (by contrast, Jacob and his family are described as "going down" into Egypt). In modern times, it has also come to mean migration to Israel. Youth Aliyah arranges the migration of young people, especially children who have been left without parents.

44

Most Youth Aliyah settlers live, and learn farm work, in special farming villages which they have built for themselves. In their spare time some may be members of Gadna or the Tzofim. The Tzofim are Scouts—not *Boy* Scouts, because there is no separate movement for girls. Girls join the same groups as boys. They also join in with the boys if they become members of Gadna, the Israeli Youth Corps. Gadna is rather like the Scouts, but it is run by the government for people a little above the usual age for scouting. Apart from first steps in military training, their main activity is pioneering work—helping to improve land that is still too poor for farming. When they are called up for compulsory military service they may join a group called Nahal, or Young Fighter-Pioneers. Nahal members spend only the first few months of their service in military training. After that, they go out to open up new farmland and farm settlements along the borders, where they can also help to protect Israel against invaders.

Some of them stay in the settlements, or go to similar ones, when their compulsory military service is over. But most return to more comfortable areas, and join in the ordinary life of developed Israel. Now let us see what kind of life that is.

Living in Israel

The word Jewish has two meanings. It can be used to describe both a nation and a religion. And people sometimes forget that there is a difference between the two. When they hear that the state of Israel is the homeland of the Jewish nation, they imagine that the Jewish religion controls the state. But they are mistaken. Neither the Jewish religion nor any other religion has any direct part in the government of Israel, and people who belong to the Jewish religion have no special privileges. However, most Israelis are Jews by religion as well as by nationality, so the rules of the Jewish religion have done much towards setting the pattern of their daily life.

The most noticeable part of the pattern is *Shabbat*—Sabbath

Children wearing traditional skullcaps worn by religious Jews

in English—the weekly holy day. Christians have made Sunday their Sabbath; for Jews, Shabbat is the seventh day of the week, Saturday. It is a day that they take very seriously, more seriously than the strictest of Christians take Sunday. All places of business and entertainment are closed. Public transport stops. Among the religious people, no work of any kind is done. That includes cooking and any other preparation of food. After a special meal on Friday evening, religious Jews eat only cold or previously prepared food until Shabbat ends at sundown on Saturday.

People of other religions are not obliged to keep Shabbat; though, of course, the general shutdown can affect them in their work and their home life. If they are Muslims or Christians they keep their own Sabbaths—Muslims on Friday, Christians on Sunday—which makes a very long weekend if you happen to be in an area where people of all three faiths live together.

Some other Jewish holy days are much more festive and less restrained than Shabbat. Many of them are public holidays. The brightest and merriest is undoubtedly Purim, which comes in March. Purim honours the memory of Esther, an exiled Jewish woman who in Bible times married a Persian king and saved a large group of fellow-exiles from death. But it also marks the coming of spring. And like spring festivals in other Mediterranean countries it is a time of carnival processions and dancing in the streets. The dancers are mainly children in fancy costume.

A street carnival on
Purim

Near the opposite end of the year comes Hanuka, also a special occasion for children. Hanuka celebrates another important event of Bible times—the rededication of the temple at the end of the successful Maccabean revolt against Greek rulers who tried to destroy the Jewish religion. The celebrations last for eight days which sometimes overlap Christmas and, like Christmas, they are a time for merry-making and present-giving. Hanuka is a time for candles. In their homes and in the synagogue, people light one candle on the eve of the first day, two candles on the eve of the second, and so on throughout the week. The candles are placed in an eight-

48

branched version of the sacred seven-branched candlestick which was lost when the Romans destroyed the temple in Jerusalem, and which is now the symbol of the state of Israel. They commemorate the single jug of oil which remained untainted in the temple after the defeat of the Greeks and which, miraculously, provided light for eight whole days.

All told, there are about forty public holidays in the Israeli year. Not all of them are Jewish or religious, nor are they all taken by everybody. If anybody tried to take them all he might easily miss some through getting his dates mixed up, because Israel has four different calendars—one Jewish, one Muslim and two Christian. Each calendar begins the new year and each new month on a different date. The Christian calendars give you two Christmas Days and two Easters. And, while the two Christian calendars agree about the number of the year, the Jewish and Muslim calendars have it differently. According to the Muslim calendar, the Christian year 1984 is 1404; and according to the Jewish calendar, it is 5744. However, all that causes no serious confusion. For everyday purposes, Israel works by one calendar only—the modern Christian calendar used in western Europe and the English-speaking countries.

In spite of their many public holidays, most Israelis work very hard. They must work very hard if they are to keep developing their country, raising their standard of living, and meeting the needs of defence at the same time. So there is usually no problem in finding work for new settlers. In fact,

Sounding the ram's horn to herald the Jewish New Year. This picture was taken on Mount Zion, in Jerusalem

work sometimes has to wait while new settlers are being trained to do it.

Because Israel is trying to grow all her own food, many new settlers go to farms and farming villages. But most Israelis live and work in towns. Visitors are often surprised to find that large numbers of them are employed by their trade union.

The union is called the *Histadrut*, which simply means the Organization. It took that name when the modern Jewish settlements had just begun, and it still needs no other, because nine out of every ten Israeli workers—including Arabs—

belong to it or to a few smaller unions linked with it. When it started, there was not much work in Palestine for Jewish immigrants. Many had skills that were being wasted. Many others were anxious to work but unsuited to the life of pioneer farm settlements. So the Histadrut set out to make work for its members and, in doing that, became one of Israel's biggest industrial and business organizations, employing over fifty thousand people. They work in foundries and timber-mills and food-processing factories, at building and engineering and quarrying, in marketing and banking and transport by land, sea and air. To its one million members who have other employers, the Histadrut offers services which workers outside

The Histadrut offers medical services in clinics like this one

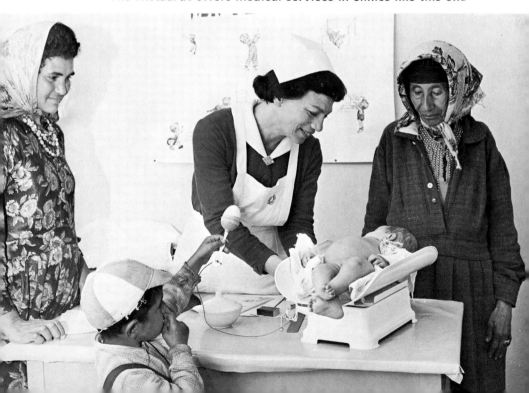

Israel do not usually expect from their trade unions. It provides what is very nearly a complete national health service. It runs evening schools and work-training centres, homes for old people and orphans, kindergartens, summer holiday-camps for children, and a travelling library. It also arranges entertainment for farm settlements, and supports no less than three hundred sports-clubs. But, of course, its main concern is to make sure that Israeli workers have fair wages and good working conditions. Through it, they have achieved wages and conditions far above those of workers in other countries of the Middle East.

However, their wages are now not so high as they might seem to somebody unused to Israeli money. Israel's currency unit is the shekel, and the inflation rate has recently become so high that Israelis expect their shekel to buy very little—perhaps even less in the near future. So a visitor need not feel extravagant if he has to pay what seems a very large number of shekels to stamp a short letter home, or an enormous number for a simple lunch in a dairy restaurant.

In the dairy restaurant the main foods on the menu will not, as might be expected, consist only of dairy products. They will include various kinds of fish—usually very good fish, fresh from the Sea of Galilee or the Mediterranean, or from artificial ponds in which they are farmed. The reason is that food is another point where the rules of the Jewish religion shape the pattern of daily life. The rules go back to early Bible times. Many seem to have begun for good practical reasons—often reasons to do with health and hygiene. But nowadays some of them may seem a little odd, even to Jewish people. Many Israelis no longer keep to them, especially in their own homes. However, most hotels and other public eating-places do keep to them. So visitors often find themselves in restaurants where milk—even in a cup of tea or coffee—or other dairy products are never served with meat from an animal or bird. If they want milk or cheese or a pudding with cream, they must go to a dairy restaurant and have it with fish. If they go to a private house, they may find that the kitchen has an unusually large stock of saucepans and other equipment. People who keep to the rules never use the same equipment for dairy products and meat.

Should the visitors call between meals, they may well be offered *pitta* and *taheena*, or a *felafel*. Pitta is bread made without yeast, and baked in flat slabs about the size of a pancake. Taheena is a paste made of sesame seeds, ground up and flavoured with garlic. You either spread the taheena over a slab of pitta, or break the pitta up and dip pieces into the taheena. Pitta is also used to make a felafel. You break a slab in half, and use the halves to sandwich fried balls made of chickpeas, ground up and mixed with peppers, pickles and spices. Because felafel is often sold hot from street stalls, it has been called Israel's answer to the hot-dog. And it is a very good answer. Hot-dog sellers would find business very slack if there was felafel about in other countries.

Pitta, taheena and felafel are not special Israeli foods. They were brought into Israel from Arab countries. And such "typically Israeli" dishes as *blintzes* (stuffed pancakes) and *hamantaschen* (three-cornered sweet pastries eaten at Purim) are really European Jewish foods, brought to Israel by settlers. So far, Israel has not invented a recipe that is really its own, but it makes up for that by the variety and quality of its fruit and vegetables.

Fruit and vegetables—as well as other locally-produced foods—are also fairly cheap. Israelis are glad of that, because the general cost of living is high. Taxes are high, too. They must be while large sums of money are needed for defence. That is one reason why most Israeli homes are small. In towns, most homes are flats, in buildings made of stone or reinforced concrete—Israel has plenty of building stone, and also plenty of the raw materials which are used to make cement for concrete. Floors, too, are made of stone or tile, usually un-covered except for a mat here and there, and so can be clammy and cold to bare feet on a winter morning. But Israelis are less concerned with cold than with heat. They have so much more of that. Their homes are designed to shut out heat and the things that go with it—insects and the gritty dust that is very easily stirred, and sometimes drifts in from the deserts on a hot wind called the *sharav*. So windows are usually screened with plastic or wire mesh and blinds, and often with shutters too.

Not that Israelis like shutting themselves in. They are very much an outdoor people, fond of picnics and hiking and talking

Tel Aviv's Carmel Market where locally grown produce can be bought at very cheap prices

over coffee at the tables of pavement cafés. Outdoor games are also very popular, especially soccer, athletics, basketball and swimming. As many as eight thousand swimmers compete in an annual five-kilometre (three-mile) race across the south-east corner of the warm Sea of Galilee. And children from all schools can take tests in games and athletics which may win them the national sports badge.

But apart from that, about one-fifth of Israel's people lead outdoor lives on farms and in farming settlements. And for a modern industrial nation, one-fifth is a fairly big fraction—certainly big enough for us to take a look at country life.

Kibbutzniks and Others

In 1909, nearly forty years before the state of Israel was founded, twelve young Jews from Europe pitched tents in the valley of the River Jordan, at the southern end of the Sea of Galilee. They were all under twenty years old. They had very little money, and very little of anything else except determination to make a piece of the promised land "flow with milk and honey". The piece they had chosen could hardly have looked less promising. Misuse and neglect had turned it into a smelly swamp, infested by the mosquitoes that carry malaria. They called it *Degania*, a name made up from the Hebrew word for corn. In time—after years of daunting work and personal suffering—they made it grow corn. They also made it grow a way of life—the kibbutz way of life which has been the main reason for Israel's speedy success in pioneer farming, and is now followed by more than one hundred thousand Israelis in over two hundred and sixty settlements.

Nowadays, people speak of each settlement as a *kibbutz*, or of *kibbutzim* if they use the proper Hebrew plural. And they call the settlers kibbutzniks. But it is really the kibbutzniks who are the kibbutz. Kibbutz means group. And the first principle of a kibbutz settlement is that its members act as a group. They share all the work equally, and they also have equal shares in planning the work and in what the work produces.

When a settlement is beginning, the settlers usually live in tents, like the first kibbutzniks at Degania. But, as they find time and money, they build more solid homes, comfortable

A kibbutz bride and groom. Like all kibbutz members, this couple will have no dining-room or full-sized kitchen in their own house. Their meals are provided in the kibbutz dining-room and are cooked and eaten communally

though simple, and not very spacious. Even married couples rarely have more than two rooms. But then they never need a dining-room or a full-size kitchen. Kibbutzniks usually share their meals as well as their work. The food is prepared in the kibbutz kitchen, and eaten in a communal dining-room that is also used for concerts, plays, film-shows and business meetings.

Married kibbutzniks may also need very little room for their children, because often young kibbutzniks do not live with their parents. From the age of eleven at Degania, but from much lower ages—even babyhood—in most other kibbutzim, they sleep and spend most of their time in special children's quarters, and are at home for the whole day only on Shabbat and public holidays.

To live in the children's quarters is rather like being at a boarding-school in your own backyard. The children sleep in small dormitories, take their meals together and have common playrooms. But the older ones often go away for lessons to a high school shared by several kibbutzim. All the children do a daily share of the kibbutz work—helping in the fields or around the houses—when lessons are over.

Some Israelis do not approve of the Kibbutz arrangements for children. Like most Jews everywhere, they are strongly attached to family life, and feel that there is not enough of it in kibbutz settlements. But the kibbutzim could not have been nearly so successful if mothers had been left to prepare family meals and look after their children instead of taking a full share in general kibbutz work. And the children do not seem to mind living apart from their parents, since they are used to it from a very early age. At any rate, many people who have grown up in kibbutzim keep to the kibbutz life, and bring up their own children in the same way.

As a kibbutz grows, it sometimes finds that it has more members than are needed to work the land, tend the animals and keep the community going. So it may add fishing or fish-breeding to farming, or perhaps start a factory of some kind. Kibbutzim are now canning food, making plywood and furniture and metal goods, and even assembling motor-scooters. Others, like the kibbutz at Ein Gev on the eastern

Fishing on the Sea of Galilee

shore of the Sea of Galilee, have found different ways of expanding their activities. Ein Gev has become famous for its waterside restaurant, which serves Galilee fish caught minutes before you eat them. It is even more famous as a centre for serious music. Great musicians come from all over the world to give concerts at its spring festival. Visitors can enjoy not only the fish and the festival but also a seaside holiday, camping among the Australian gumtrees in the kibbutz camping-ground.

Visitors can spend holidays in other kibbutzim, too. Twenty of them run comfortable guest-houses. But, whatever a kibbutz may do to occupy its members, every kibbutznik gets exactly the same reward for his work. And he does not get it in money. Instead, he is given a credit card which allows him to take what he wants, or to order what he wants, from the kibbutz stores. That can include anything from a bedstead to a block of chocolate, so a kibbutznik really has no need of money in his daily life. However, he must leave his kibbutz sometimes, and then he can change some of his kibbutz credit into money for use outside.

The "no money" system is another reason why many Israelis do not join the kibbutzim. They feel that there is more freedom of choice when you can shop where you want to, and perhaps have money over to invest or put in a bank. But they do like the kibbutz idea of sharing work and sharing rewards—the co-operative system as it is usually called—and so they have chosen a life that is somewhere between the lives of the kibbutznik and the independent farmer. They live in villages where each family has its own home and usually its own farmland, but co-operates with the other families in planning the work, buying and using equipment, and selling produce. Sometimes too the farmers hold the land co-operatively, and work it in the kibbutz way as one big farm. All these villages are called *moshavim*, and there are in fact a good many more of them than there are of kibbutzim.

Israel has its independent farmers, too, especially in the orange-growing industry. Oranges and other citrus fruits are by far the biggest of Israel's farm crops, and most of her 89,000 hectares (220,000 acres) of citrus groves are cultivated by independent farmers who sell their crops through a government marketing board. That is why all Israeli oranges are

60

stamped with the name *Jaffa*. There is in fact a town called Jaffa—a very old one in the coastal area that was once the home of the Philistines. The orange-growing industry began on some farms near by about a hundred years ago. And nowadays the government marketing board uses *Jaffa* as a brand-name for Israel's entire citrus crop. So your Jaffa orange may well have been picked on a smallholding near Haifa, or a kibbutz by the Sea of Galilee.

The independent citrus farmers are mainly Jewish. But a large number of Israel's Arabs are also independent farmers.

Market day at Beersheba, the capital of the Negev. The camels belong to local Bedouin Arabs

Most of them have small farms in the green and beautiful hill country above the Sea of Galilee, where they grow grain and tobacco, fruit and vegetables and olives. In their ways of working and living—and sometimes even in their clothes—they are much more like the "Bible pictures" than their Jewish fellow-citizens. They have the same rights and privileges as the Jews; and, with education, welfare services and government help in farm improvement, they have become much more prosperous and healthy than they were before they became Israelis.

Over twenty thousand of Israel's "country Arabs" live at the

A Bedouin with his sheep

opposite end of the country, in the desert areas of the Negev. Most can hardly be called farmers because—like Abraham of the Bible—they live mainly a nomadic life, moving their black tents and their sheep and goats from pasture to pasture and from well to well. The pastures are sometimes scanty. The wells are sometimes dry or at best low and muddy. In recent years, some of the Bedouin have decided that it is much more comfortable to live a settled life in or around the towns that are fast developing in the Negev. They work as labourers in the building industry or on roads, and a few are beginning to take jobs in the new factories of the new towns—factories which make pottery, glassware and chemicals from Negev minerals.

However, many go back to their black goat-hair tents at night. And those who keep completely to the old way of life have the benefit of Israel's travelling medical service and a water supply that is much more reliable than natural wells. It comes through huge pipes—some of them three metres (nine feet) in diameter—from the Sea of Galilee and the Yarkon River near Tel Aviv. It has already made farmland of part of the Negev, and farmers of some Bedouin Arabs.

This Year in Jerusalem

People who talk about Jerusalem often quote an old Jewish saying: "Of ten portions of beauty given to the world, Jerusalem had nine, and the rest of the world only one."

It is easy to understand why they do so. In its own special way and its high rockbound setting, Jerusalem is a beautiful city. But the saying continues: "Of ten portions of sorrow sent down on the world, nine fell on Jerusalem." And that sentence is much nearer the truth than the one about beauty. No city has seen so much sorrow over so many centuries. Nor does any city show the marks of its sorrow so clearly.

Outstanding among those marks is the site of the temple, a vast rectangular courtyard covering the levelled top of a hill. About eight hectares (twenty acres) in area, it fills in the south-east corner of the wall enclosing the Old City, and is supported on the western side by the massive stone blocks of a much older wall, more than twenty metres (sixty feet) high. Most of this western support wall is now hidden by houses, but you can walk along the foot of the rest. And there you will always find religious Jews with their faces towards the stones, praying. Many will be dressed in the traditional clothes of Jews from eastern Europe—long black coats or striped gowns, with broad-brimmed hats that are sometimes thickly trimmed with fur. Others will be wearing ordinary European city clothes, or the open-necked shirt and slacks of kibbutzniks, or army uniform, or the headdress and perhaps the robe of Arab

64

Crowds praying at the Western Wall—all that remains of the Jerusalem temple, destroyed by the Romans in A.D. 70

countries. To all of them the Western Wall—sometimes called the Wailing Wall—is the holiest of all holy places. It represents the temple destroyed by the Romans and the earlier temple of Solomon, both of which stood on the levelled hilltop above. And it is all that remains of either.

For century after century, religious Jews have come to the Wall to pray, often after perilous travel among unfriendly people. But they were forbidden even that during the first nineteen years of the existence of the State of Israel, when the Old City was held by Israel's Arab neighbour Jordan. Many of them also lost their homes. Until 1948, Muslims, Christians

65

and Jews had shared the Old City, each community following its own way of life in its own separate quarter, with no serious interference from the others. But, in the fighting of that year, the Arab invaders destroyed much of the Jewish quarter. Later, when all the surviving Jews had been removed, the rest of their houses and synagogues (Jewish churches) were knocked down. And no Jews were allowed into the Old City—or into the Jordan side of the New City—until Israel occupied the whole area in the war of 1967.

Since then, the Jewish quarter has come to life again. And it is now possible to stand back and look at the Western Wall instead of craning your neck in the alley which used to run between it and some old buildings. As for the Moslem and Christian quarters, they are still where they were, and will remain so, as Israel intends to keep the Old City and the other holy places of Jerusalem freely open to people of all religions.

The Christian quarter is centred on the great three-domed Church of the Holy Sepulchre, which is believed to stand over the places where Jesus was crucified and buried. That does not mean that the Bible is wrong in saying that the place of crucifixion lay outside the wall of the Old City. The present city wall was built by the Turks, and encloses a wider area than the wall of Roman times. Since Roman times there have also been changes in street levels. The road which led from the grim Antonia fortress where Jesus was tried—at present a school—to the place of crucifixion is now about ten feet (three metres) underground. Christian pilgrims follow its line by

Christian pilgrims at prayer before following the route of the crucifixion along the Via Dolorosa

walking along a street with the Latin name Via Dolorosa, which means Sorrowful Road.

East of the Holy Sepulchre spreads the main market area, and the Moslem quarter which is much like everybody's idea of an Arab city—winding shadowy alleys, noisy bazaars, veiled women, craftsmen working with metals and leather against a background of oriental music. Some of the narrow market lanes have changed very little in the seven hundred years since Christian Crusaders ruled Jerusalem. The Crusaders' name for one lane is still remembered. They called it Bad Cooking Street—which was perhaps hardly fair to the Arab stallholders if the foods on sale looked as tasty then as they can do today.

67

There has been a Muslim community—usually a very large one—in Jerusalem since the Muslim religion spread into Palestine in A.D. 638. Like their Christian neighbours, the Muslims have great reverence for the prophets, teachers and holy places of the Jewish religion. They believe that their own prophet Mohammed ascended to heaven from a rock which marks the place where the altar of the temple stood. For that reason, the early Arab rulers made the temple site a Muslim sanctuary, and built two magnificent mosques (Muslim churches) on it. One, called the Dome of the Rock, is a huge eight-sided building with walls of green and blue tiles and a dome that now glistens with a new sheathing of gold-coloured aluminium. It stands near the centre of the temple site, with the rock of the ancient altar in its own centre. The other mosque, the silver-domed El Aqsa, is even bigger, and has the rectangular shape of many Christian churches. It fills in much of the southern end of the temple site, the end overlooking the Valley of Kidron which is often mentioned in the Bible, and the grey stone houses of a fast-developing section of the New City.

New City is perhaps a misleading name for the part of Jerusalem which spreads widely over the rocky hills and valleys around the Old City. Some of it is quite as ancient as the Old City, and it contains buildings and areas which are almost as important to pilgrims and students of Bible history as the Old City's holy places. There is the Mount of Olives, with the ancient Jewish cemetery and the Garden of Gethsemane on its slopes, and on its crest the place from which, in the Christian

68

belief, Jesus ascended to heaven. There is Mount Zion, with King David's tomb below the room where Jesus and his disciples ate their last supper together. There are in every direction other monuments and names and buildings that recall the Bible and the long sorry story of Jerusalem in the centuries after Bible times. But the New City also contains the railway station, the bus station, the main post office, the modern shopping centre, and the square, flat-roofed, very twentieth-century building from which the Knesset's one hundred and twenty members govern the State of Israel. It has to contain them, and not only because the Old City was cut off from Israel between 1948 and 1967. Another very practical reason is that there has been no room for new buildings in the Old City for many years. As far back as 1827, a suburb outside the wall was built for poor Jews of the Yishuv who had been living unsheltered in the Old City's streets. It was paid for by Sir Moses Montefiore, a member of a famous family of British Jews. And the New City has been growing ever since.

It is not an industrial city. Nor is it a commercial centre. Industry and commerce grow where raw materials are easily obtained and goods easily transported. Jerusalem has never met those needs. It became the capital of Israel because of its meaning, its place as the ancient centre of Jewish life. It is now the centre of Israeli life—the seat of the president and parliament; of the civil service and the legal system; of organizations like the Jewish Agency which not only bring settlers to Israel but also improve and develop areas where they may live and work; of the Hebrew University where about twelve thousand Israelis receive advanced education and work on research in all the arts and sciences, and of the National Museum which contains, among a vast collection of ancient and modern treasures, the famous early Bible manuscripts known as the Dead Sea Scrolls. It is also, of course, the main centre for tourists and pilgrims. Jerusalem remains, as it always has been, the first aim of every visitor.

So the stone villas and bungalows and the concrete blocks of flats spreading up and over the Jerusalem hills are mainly the

The Dome of the Rock—this mosque stands on the site of the Jewish temple

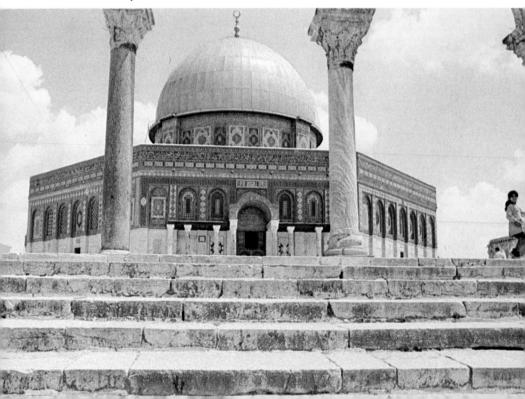

New apartment buildings in Jerusalem

homes of government workers, of scholars and teachers and students and local business people. To find a centre of industry and commerce, we must take the railway or the hilly Jaffa road westward and down through the orange groves and vineyards of the coastal lowlands to a really new city—the city of Tel Aviv.

The Other Cities, and Some Towns

For its first fifteen years as a city, Tel Aviv had as its mayor the man who had founded it. His name was Meir Dizengoff. And one of the many stories told about him is that he liked to answer the question "How many people has your city?" by saying "Do you want this morning's figure, or will you wait for this afternoon's?"

That is not such a great exaggeration as it may seem. There really were times when Tel Aviv's population increased noticeably during a single day. In sixty years, it has grown from about two hundred to well over a million. The two hundred

Modern Tel Aviv, Israel's largest city

were a group of families, mainly immigrants from Europe, who had been living in the neighbouring seaport town of Jaffa. Jaffa, largely an Arab town, was overcrowded, uncomfortable and not very clean. So the Jewish families—inspired by Meir Dizengoff—bought some wasteland among the sand-dunes north of the town, called it *Tel Aviv*, which means Hill of Spring, and built themselves a double row of small houses. The space between the houses they called Herzl Street, after the founder of the Zionist Movement. Before their younger children had grown up, Herzl Street was the heart of a city as big as its neighbour Jaffa. By the time their grandchildren had grown up, Tel Aviv was the biggest city in Israel. Jaffa had become its southern suburb. Visitors looking for Herzl Street could use its thirty-five-storey skyscraper as a landmark.

Perhaps because it has grown up so quickly, Tel Aviv seems to live quickly. It is a bright, bustling, wideawake city, a city which matches the character of the sabra Israelis—pushing on the surface, but kindly underneath. It is also a city whose people seem less concerned with the traditional Jewish way of life than most Israelis. If you want to eat a lamb chop and drink milk at the same meal, it is easy to find a restaurant in Tel Aviv that serves them together. And a Tel Aviv Shabbat seems more like a holiday than a holy day. Thousands of strollers and swimmers and picnickers fill the beach and the boulevard along the city's waterfront, and the banks of the Yarkon River whose mouth is in the harbour area at the northern end of the city. The Yarkon is a very short river—

A view of Tel Aviv

only about fifteen miles (twenty-four kilometres) from source to
mouth—and it is now less broad and deep than it was when
Tel Aviv was founded. Much of its water is piped away to
irrigate the dry Negev.

On weekdays, many of Tel Aviv's workers are employed in
the diamond industry. Diamonds are not mined in Israel, but
every year a vast quantity of rough diamonds is imported for
the delicate and difficult tasks of cutting and polishing. They
are then exported, mainly to the jewel markets of the U.S.A.
and eastern Asia. Other workers help to turn out the factory
products, ranging from electronic equipment to powdered
soup, which make Tel Aviv a very important industrial city.
But its commercial importance is greater. Apart from being the

chief marketing and general business centre for the southern half of the country, it has the head offices of most major national business organizations, and of most foreign organizations that are represented in Israel. The international airport at Lod, about ten miles (sixteen kilometres) inland, has done much to make it the centre of foreign business; and, since 1965, a new artificially constructed seaport at the old Philistine town of Ashdod, twenty miles (thirty-two kilometres) to the south, has greatly expanded its sea trade. Its own harbour was too small for the increasing traffic, and has now been closed to commercial shipping.

It is not only the opportunities in commerce and industry that bring people to Tel Aviv. The city is also Israel's main centre for entertainment of all kinds, from the serious music of the Israel Symphony Orchestra and the serious plays of the National Theatre to night clubs and the Purim Carnival. Tel Aviv's Purim Carnival has the longest and most spectacular processions in the country, and also the biggest and noisiest crowds of street dancers, most of whom try to jam themselves into Mograbi Square, where the main street opens out before it goes down to the waterfront boulevard.

Some of Tel Aviv's entertainment has spilled over into Jaffa, which is no longer an Arab town. During the last months of British rule, it became a base for Arab attacks on Tel Aviv. Serious fighting broke out and, as a result, the British moved most of the Jaffa Arabs to other areas, and they did not come back when the State of Israel was founded. Their place has since been taken by Jews who have recently settled in Israel, including some of the "Magic Carpet" immigrants.

Jaffa is a very ancient town. It is also one of the oldest seaports known to history, although its harbour—like Tel Aviv's —is now closed to commercial shipping. Some of its domed houses and narrow cobbled lanes remain as they have been for centuries, but perhaps it interests visitors mainly because of its connection with four famous stories.

It was from the harbour of Jaffa, then called Joppa, that Jonah of the Old Testament began the voyage on which he was thrown overboard and swallowed by a whale. It was in one of the small domed houses that the apostle Peter of the New Testament revived the charitable dressmaker Dorcas, who appeared to be dead. And it was on a large rock off the seafront —still called Andromeda's Rock—that Perseus of Greek mythology killed a monster who was about to eat the girl Andromeda.

The fourth story links Jaffa with Lod, the international airport town. Lod used to be, and sometimes still is, called by the Greek name Lydda. And at Lydda, in early Christian times, a soldier named Georgios was martyred. After a few centuries of changing faiths and changing peoples, his story became mixed up with the Jaffa story of Perseus. When the Christian Crusaders came to Palestine they were told that Georgios had killed the monster on Andromeda's Rock. The English Crusaders were particularly pleased with the story. They made Georgios their patron saint, and later, under the

76

English form of his name, he became St. George, the patron saint of England.

Lod, now the centre of Israel's aircraft industry as well as her international airport, is also connected with St. Peter. The New Testament says that he stopped there on his way to Jaffa, and cured a man who was seriously ill. It also tells us that, from Jaffa, Peter went north to Caesarea through the richly fertile Plain of Sharon, which has given us the flower name "rose of Sharon", and also a popular girl's name—unfortunately often mispronounced. The towns that he passed through are not mentioned, but he certainly would not have seen Petah Tikvah,

A concert in the partially restored amphitheatre at Caesarea

Herzliya, Natanya or Hadera. Those towns, and many villages further inland, have been founded in modern times by Jewish settlers. The first group arrived in the 1870s, and found that the Plain of Sharon was no longer the kindly farmland of their ancestors. The lower levels were marshy, the higher levels smothered by sand. Some of the plain is still like that. But over most of it the hard-working settlers have now brought back the good red soil of Bible times. They grow fodder for dairy cattle, and much of the fruit that Israel exports to colder countries.

Caesarea, on the coast near the northern edge of the plain, could be called the Tel Aviv of Roman Palestine. Founded and built during the reign of Herod, the ruthless and unpopular puppet king of the Christmas story, it was named by him after

Crusader arches in Caesarea

the Roman emperor Augustus Caesar, and became the centre of Roman life and commerce. But the early Arab invaders of Palestine had no use for such cities. After centuries of slow decay, it was destroyed during the Crusades, and was little more than a partly buried mass of ruins until the Israelis revived it as a seaside tourist and golfing resort, set against a background of banana plantations.

Caesarea had a great artificial harbour that is unlikely to be revived. Nor is the harbour of Acre, about thirty miles (forty-eight kilometres) northward. As a seaport, Acre is at least as old as Jaffa. It is said to be the place where glass was invented. It certainly grew rich by using and exporting a purple cloth dye made from a shellfish found locally. Later, it became the commercial capital of Crusader Palestine.

Some of the Crusader walls and buildings are still there. So too are mosques and minarets and a fortress from Turkish times. The Israelis have added an extensive industrial quarter with much new housing. But the harbour is no longer important. Nowadays, the seaport for all northern Israel is the country's third city, Haifa.

Unlike Acre and Jaffa, Haifa is a new seaport. It is also a new city. Hardly more than a small coastal town when the Turks ruled Palestine, it became a port for deep-water shipping under the British who followed them, and a major centre of industry and commerce under the Israelis. It is also, of course, the main market and outlet for the farm produce of Galilee and much of the Plain of Sharon.

A view of Acre showing the old Crusader walls

With one exception, Haifa's most noticeable buildings are industrial and commercial—the oil refineries, the foundries and office blocks, the great skyscraper grain silo. The one exception is the tall gold-domed shrine of the Bahai religion, founded by a Persian who spent much of his life in the Turkish prison at Acre. The Bahai religion is centred on Haifa but most of its members live in other countries.

The Druze religion is also represented in Haifa. Originally Muslims, the Druze developed a religion of their own and live as a separate self-governing community but with full Israeli citizenship. The baggy-trousered, thick-moustached Druze men are outstanding horsemen and fighters, and have played an important part in the defence of Israel. They live in the northern part of the country, in about twenty farming villages between Mount Carmel, which looks down on Haifa, and Mount Hermon on the north-east frontier.

In spite of Jerusalem's claim, visitors are usually inclined to choose Haifa as Israel's most beautiful city. The reason is not the city itself, but the seaward flank of Mount Carmel sloping down to the broad blue bay. Haifa's two main residential districts are both on Mount Carmel. One spreads over the slopes, around the Bahai shrine and its huge and colourful Persian garden. The other lies along the pine-wooded crest. Both may be reached by a funicular railway which climbs straight up from the commercial district at shore level. Also on

A Druze shopkeeper and his son

A view of Haifa Bay from Mount Carmel

the crest are Israel's technological university and a Christian monastery whose patron saint is Elijah of the Old Testament. It was on Mount Carmel that a disastrous drought ended after Elijah had prayed for rain.

Mount Carmel is a range of mountains rather than a single peak. Its ridges extend about fifteen miles (twenty-four kilometres) inland from Haifa. At some points along them it is possible to see across the whole of north Israel to the snowy crest of Mount Hermon.

Far North to Far South

According to a Jewish folk story, God first intended Mount Hermon to be very small, and he made it so. But when huge Mount Sinai in the far south was chosen as the place for Moses to receive the Ten Commandments, Mount Hermon began to weep. So God took pity on the miserable little mountain. He made it the highest peak in the land of Israel, and let its tears become the headwaters of the Jordan, Israel's longest river.

It may be true that Mount Hermon was once smaller than it is now. There was certainly volcanic activity in the area a very long time ago. One result of it was a blockage of the River

A waterpipe for irrigation and general water supply in the Jordan Valley

Jordan, which left a small lake and a large swamp in the Huleh Valley at the foot of the mountain. But you will not find Lake Huleh on a modern map of Israel. In the 1950s, engineers enlarged the Jordan south of the lake to make it carry the lake water and most of the swamp water down to the Sea of Galilee. As a result, Israel now has another twenty square miles (about fifty square kilometres) of fertile land.

The rest of the Huleh Valley always had been fertile. It was the home of the northern Hebrew tribe of Dan in Bible times. And it attracted several groups of immigrants in the early days of modern settlement. Though the soil was good, life was not easy for them. The valley was roadless, and remote from towns or other settlement areas. Mosquitoes from the swamps spread malaria. And, because the valley lay close to an unfriendly country, there was constant danger of attack. One small

Draining the swamps of the Huleh Valley

settlement, Tel Hai, was completely destroyed by attackers in 1920—but not until its "army" of six men and two women had all been killed in a gallant attempt to hold it. Their leader was a one-armed Russian Jew named Josef Trumpeldor. And Israel now keeps an annual public holiday, Tel Hai Day, in memory of him and his small company. On Tel Hai Day many Israelis, mainly young people, make a pilgrimage to the stone lion which stands as a memorial at the new Tel Hai.

Some of the pilgrims stay at the Tel Hai youth hostel or at the now safe and successful settlements in the area. Many take the opportunity to visit the Huleh Wildlife Reserve. Before the swamp was drained, it was very thickly populated with wild-life, mainly waterbirds. Part of it was left undrained as a permanent reserve for them. There are other wildlife reserves in several parts of Israel, and visitors are sometimes surprised to find that they contain not only a wide variety of smaller creatures, but also wild boars, jackals, hyenas, wolves and leopards.

The work of draining the Huleh Valley was arranged and paid for by the Jewish National Fund, which works with the Jewish Agency to make the poorer soil of Israel productive and fit for settlement. It has vastly increased the country's farm-land, planted extensive forests in many areas, and built roads throughout the country.

Many of the trees have been planted in the eroded areas of the Jordan Valley, which runs down the eastern side of Israel from the Sea of Galilee to the Dead Sea. The valley includes

Planting saplings which will grow into a pine forest—a JNF project

the wilderness of Judaea, so often mentioned in the Bible. Until the war of 1967, most of it lay outside the boundaries of Israel. Nineteen years before, the kingdom of Jordan had taken a huge bite from the territory west of the river, leaving Israel without some of the most ancient Jewish parts of the promised land. The bite took in the oasis city of Jericho, where the Hebrews crossed the Jordan after their captivity in Egypt, and which now calls itself the oldest city in the world. It took in Bethlehem, now a crowded Arab town with a large and not very attractive Christian church built over a cave-stable

86

which may be the stable of the Christmas story. It took in Hebron where Abraham lived and is buried, and Samaria the centre of the old northern kingdom. And it took in Qumran, where the Dead Sea Scrolls were found in some of the caves which make a vast wasp's nest of the rocky hills above the Dead Sea.

The whole bite has now come back to Israel. As the River Jordan makes a clear natural boundary between Israel and the kingdom of Jordan, there is good reason for her wishing to keep it. However, most of its people are Arabs. And their wishes and interests will certainly be considered when Israel and her neighbours can at last get down to talks about "a just and lasting peace".

The Dead Sea, forty-six miles (seventy-three kilometres) from north to south, continues the frontier between Israel and the kingdom of Jordan, and Israel now controls the entire western half. Like the Sea of Galilee, it is really a lake. Also like the Sea of Galilee, it lies below sea-level. But the Dead Sea is twice as far down as the Sea of Galilee. It is, in fact, the lowest point on the earth's surface, nearly thirteen hundred feet (390 metres) below the level of the Mediterranean shore about fifty miles (eighty kilometres) to the west.

Once the waters of the Jordan have come into the Dead Sea, their flow stops. There is no way out except by evaporation. That means that all the salts and other minerals that they have picked up on their way down from Mount Hermon stay in the Dead Sea, making it much more salty than any other salt water. One result is that the most timid bather need have no fear of sinking. He may lie on the water and read a newspaper if he wishes. The water will hold him up as long as he cares to stay in it. Another result is that, by evaporating Dead Sea water, Israel can draw on a vast and constantly restocking supply of useful chemicals. Because the Dead Sea area is so hot, evaporation is no trouble at all. Along the shores, huge pillars and banks of salt have piled up without any help from man. One of the pillars is said to be the wife of Lot, Abraham's nephew. In the Old Testament story of the destruction of Sodom and Gomorrah, she was turned into a pillar of salt when she disobeyed the angels who told her not to look back as she fled with Lot and their children from the doomed city.

Nowadays, Sodom is making its own pillars of salt. Near the site of the destroyed city are the Dead Sea Chemical Works, at which man is hastening the natural evaporation process, and extracting the Dead Sea's minerals both for export and for Israel's own use. Modern Sodom consists of nothing but the chemical works. The workers are brought down daily from Arad and Dimona, two new towns on the Negev plateau above. Arad aims to have a population of fifty thousand or more employed in factories using Negev materials. It has been very carefully planned for comfortable living in a naturally uncomfortable area. Dimona too has its own factories and is also a centre for research into the peaceful uses of atomic energy.

The Dead Sea chemicals, with other minerals from the

Negev, are among the most valuable of Israel's exports. They are shipped from the Negev's own seaport of Eilat, at the eastern head of the Red Sea. Eilat's life as a seaport began in Bible times. King Solomon used it to export copper from the Negev mines that the Israelis have reopened, and to import the gold and the African luxuries for which his court was famous. But the site was as empty as the surrounding desert in 1948. So modern Eilat is yet another new town. The cargoes which it handles come down from Beersheba—the Negev's main town —and the other industrial areas by a newly built motor road. An airport links it with the rest of Israel. It is also linked to the refineries at Haifa by an oil pipeline. Israel's own oil-wells meet only part of her needs; the rest comes to Eilat by tanker. Visitors in search of all-the-year-round sea-bathing, skin-

Eilat, Israel's Red Sea port and holiday resort

diving over coral reefs and sunshine on practically every day of the year have also helped it to grow quickly. For some visitors, the desert kibbutzim to the north of Eilat are another point of interest. After much experiment—often painfully disappointing—they are now providing Eilat not only with fresh vegetables and eggs but also with milk from well-fed dairy cows.

Eilat is the most southerly part of Israel. But the vast and largely mountainous desert of Sinai lies between it and the western head of the Red Sea. And Israel took a great but carefully calculated risk when it returned Sinai to Egypt during the years 1980–1982. Like the Golan heights above the Huleh

Valley in the north, and the Jordan Valley area in the east, Sinai was a protective barrier between Israel proper and a possible source of invasion. It also decreased the chances of invasion and guerilla raids through a fourth piece of occupied territory, the Gaza Strip.

The Gaza Strip is a narrow belt of flat and fertile Mediterranean coastland, opposite the southern end of the Dead Sea. For anyone who occupies Sinai, it is an open corridor into Israel. Raiders made much destructive use of it before Israeli troops captured it in 1967. Among the 450,000 Arabs who live

Bedouin woman in the Sinai Desert

in the Strip, more than half are people who fled from Israel in the fighting of 1948. They were not allowed into other Arab countries, and were unwilling or unable to return to Israel when the fighting ended. So they are still refugees, living in camps with help from the United Nations Organization and, since 1967, from Israel. They, too, are part of the problem for peacemakers.

Meanwhile, Israel's chief strength seems to be that she can carry on almost as if there were no problem, to build a productive and advanced state in the face of those who wish to destroy it. She is helped by the fact that she is confident of her ability to defend herself, and also by believing that her most powerful weapon is *ein brera*. But perhaps the best hope for the future lies in the opposite side of her character. It was a prophet of the people Israel who forecast a time when . . . . . . *they shall beat their swords into ploughshares and their spears into pruning-hooks. Nation shall not lift up sword against nation, neither shall they learn war any more.*

The Israeli flag—its Star of David is a reminder of an historic past

Index

U.N.O. 27, 28, 33, 91
U.S.A. 41, 74

Via Dolorosa 67
vineyards 71
visitors (*see* tourists)
voting 36, 41, 42

wages 52
wars:
    First World 27

Second World 28
1948–49 29, 30, 75
1956 31, 32
1967 32, 66, 86
water supply 13, 22, 63, 74
welfare services 62
Western (Wailing) Wall 64, 65, 66
wilderness 12, 86
wildlife 85

Youth Aliyah 44–5